The Mighty Bears

Everyone likes to watch the bears perform at the zoo or circus. They look round and cuddly, playful and good-natured. But underneath that shaggy coat is one of the mightiest mammals on earth.

Robert McClung, former Curator of Mammals and Birds at the Bronx Zoo, introduces the reader to each member of this powerful family and tells how it lives.

Here are the North American bears—the black bear, grizzly, Alaskan brown bear, and polar bear. And here are bears from many other lands, including the bears' near-relative, the giant panda.

The Mighty Bears

by Robert M. McClung

Illustrated with photographs

 Random House · New York

For helpful suggestions about this book, the author and the publisher would like to thank Lee S. Crandall, General Curator Emeritus of the New York Zoological Park.

PHOTOGRAPH CREDITS: Myles J. Adler, 70; Alaska Pictorial Service, vi, 50, 53 top; Toni Angermayer (Photo Researchers), 65; Annan Photo Features, 62–63; George Austin (Shostal), cover; Alfred M. Bailey (National Audubon Society), 30, 53 bottom; Birnback Publishing Service, 8, 11, 52, 67, back endpaper; Black Star Publishing Co., 75; British Information Services, 28; California Historical Society, 36–37; Lynwood Chace (Outdoor Photographers League), 16; Frank and John Craighead, 42, 48, 49; Harry Engle (National Audubon Society), 20; Russ Kinne (Photo Researchers), 2; Ken Lambert (Free Lance Photographers Guild), 7; Fred J. Maroon (Photo Researchers), 72; Monkmeyer Press Photo Service, 4; Nicholas Morant (Photo-Library), 22; National Zoological Park, 29 right; Charles J. Ott (National Audubon Society), 45; Erik Parbst (Pix), 58; Ed Park (Free Lance Photographers Guild), 25; Pro Pix (Monkmeyer), 19; San Diego Zoo (Photo Researchers), 74; W. J. Schoonmaker (National Audubon Society), 33; W. Suschitzky, ii, 54, 60, 79; U.S. Department of Agriculture, Forest Service, front endpaper, 29 left; R. Van Nostrand (National Audubon Society), 77; Ylla (Rapho-Guillumette), 12, 15.

The map on page 5 is by Harry Chester. The illustration on page 39 is from *The Adventures of James Capen Adams, Mountaineer and Grizzly Bear Hunter of California* by Theodore H. Hittell (San Francisco: Towne and Bacon, 1861).

Library of Congress Catalog Card Number: 67–14438

Contents

The Mighty Bears

1. The Bear Family

Morning dew still sparkles in the grass, but the August sun shines bright and warm on the rocky hillside. Big orange and black butterflies float across the clearing. A chipmunk scurries toward his burrow, cheeks bulging with ripe blueberries. Then, from the nearby forest, a bluejay sounds its alarm call.

In a moment a shaggy black bear appears at the edge of the woods. Head up, she swings her muzzle back and forth, sniffing the air for strange odors. Satisfied, she shuffles into the meadow and heads for a clump of bushes heavy with blueberries. She

grunts softly, and two woolly cubs tumble out of the woods to join her. Soon all three of them are gulping down the juicy berries.

Rounding a thick clump of wild cherry trees, the mother bear suddenly stops with a loud "whoof!" Less than 30 feet ahead are two other berry pickers —a boy and a girl. For a long moment the bears and the children stare at each other in startled surprise. Then the mother bear snorts and wheels quickly about. Off she lumbers toward the woods, the cubs close beside her. As they disappear into the underbrush, the boy and girl start running in the opposite direction.

"Bears!" they yell to their father, farther down

4

the slope. "A big black bear and two cubs! We saw them!"

Black bears are the most common bears in North America. Yet they are seldom seen, for they are shy and usually keep hidden in wild, wooded areas. One of the best places to see them is in Yellowstone National Park in Wyoming.

Yellowstone is also the most likely place south of the Canadian border for seeing the black bear's big cousin—the legendary grizzly bear.

Besides blacks and grizzlies, two other kinds of bears live in North America. These are the big

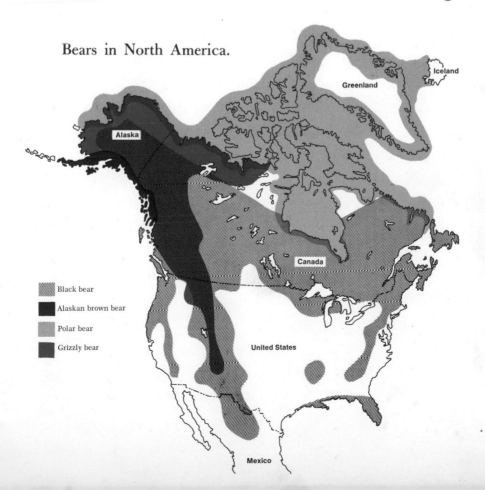

Bears in North America.

brown bears of Alaska, and the polar bears of Arctic regions. They are the giants of the bear family.

Other kinds of bears live in Europe and Asia, and one species roams the Andes Mountains of South America. There are no bears in Africa or Australia, however.

Male bears are usually quite a bit heavier than females, but all are fairly large animals. The biggest kinds sometimes weigh three-quarters of a ton or more. Even the smallest weighs about 100 pounds when full grown.

Whatever their size, bears are very strong. A big one can kill a bull with sledge-hammer blows of its mighty paws. Its powerful jaws and teeth can crunch through solid bone.

All bears have stocky bodies, tiny stub tails, and heavy, strong legs. Most of them have warm coats of thick, shaggy fur. Their heads are rather dog-like, with tapering muzzles, rounded ears, and small eyes. Most of them have rather poor eyesight. But their hearing is good, and their sense of smell is very keen.

Bears walk on the soles of their feet, as we do. American Indians sometimes called them "beasts that walk like man." Each of the bear's broad flat

6

Bears are the largest meat-eating land animals on earth.

feet has five toes; each toe is equipped with a long sharp claw.

Bears usually amble along on all four feet with a slow, shuffling gait. But when they want to they can put on surprising bursts of speed—25 or even 30 miles an hour. Sometimes they stand erect on their broad, hind feet in order to reach food, or to get a better view of whatever is in front of them. Their powerful legs make them good swimmers, too.

Most young bears, and the adults of many smaller species, are expert climbers. Hugging a tree trunk with its forelegs, the bear digs in with curved claws and goes up in a series of short bounds. Coming down, he descends rump first. Adults of the largest species do not climb, however.

Although classed as meat-eating mammals, or *carnivores,* most bears eat much more vegetable material than meat. They relish nearly all kinds of plant and animal foods—from roots and buds to the bark of trees, from tiny insects to big hoofed mammals. They fill up on whatever is easiest to get at any season. They grind up the food with their cheek teeth, which have broad, flat crowns.

Bears wander widely in search of their meals.

9

Expert climbers when young, black bears climb trees to look for honey and other food, or to escape an enemy.

Many of them have hunting ranges or territories covering many square miles. They usually travel alone, but during the summer mating season pairs of bears may stay together for a month or more. And cubs usually remain with their mother for at least a year—sometimes longer.

In temperate or cold climates, most bears do not eat anything at all during the winter. Instead, they curl up in a den and sleep through the cold months from December through March. "A bear is wiser than a man," an old Abnaki Indian of Maine once said, "because a man does not know how to live all winter without eating anything."

Bears do not fall into a very deep winter sleep, like woodchucks and other animals that hibernate. The sleeping bear's temperature remains close to normal during the winter. It breathes regularly, four or five times each minute. It frequently wakes up and shifts its position.

The cubs of most bears are born in the winter den—often in January or February. At birth they are amazingly small and helpless, and often weigh less than a pound. But when they leave the den with their mother in the spring, they are frisky and furry, and about as big as house cats.

If all goes well, they have a long life ahead of

10

A black bear in its winter den.

them. Bears in the wild often live 20 years or more. Some in zoos have lived nearly 40 years. Except for man, they have few enemies. Man has hunted bears for their meat and fur since the days of the cave dwellers. He has probably always been their principal enemy.

2. Twin Cubs Grow Up

Hemlock branches droop with snow, and the forest floor lies deep under a thick white covering. A crow calls as it flies over the treetops, and a brittle limb snaps in the freezing January air. Otherwise, the New England woods are silent and still.

Snug in her den beneath the roots of a fallen oak tree, a female black bear snoozes in comfort. Grunting sleepily, she shifts her position. A faint voice squeals in protest.

The whimper comes from one of the two tiny cubs that lie snuggled against the big bear's warm side. Just a few days old, the cubs are hardly as big as rats. There is only the faintest suggestion of hair on their pale skin. Their eyes are closed, and their tiny ears are flattened against their heads. Their legs sprawl helplessly on either side, small claws showing at the tips of the toes. At this stage the cubs cannot do much of anything except nurse and sleep.

February comes and goes, and the daily arc of the sun swings farther northward each day. Water begins to gurgle in the nearby brook, and trees show faint color at the tips of their branches. Spring is on the way.

The mother bear sleeps on, and the two cubs grow and gain strength every day. Early in March, when they are nearly six weeks old, their eyes open. Their ears develop, too, and a thick growth of woolly black fur begins to cover their bodies. By the end of March, when they are nine weeks old, they are strong and lively. They weigh almost five pounds apiece.

One day in early April one of the cubs crawls to the entrance of the den and peers out. By now the snow has almost disappeared. Buds are swelling on the forest trees, and warm spring sunlight flickers through the branches. Frogs are calling from a nearby pond. The cub tries to crawl out into this interesting world, but the mother bear seizes it gently in her jaws and pulls it back. Not yet.

Several days later the mother bear rouses and peers out of the den herself. Now the time has come.

Scrambling out of the den, she leads the cubs through the woods. She has not eaten anything since the fall before, but she is not thin. She still has a layer of fat on her back and sides, and her fur is thick and glossy.

Two cubs take a look at the world outside their den.

Tearing up an old log, a black bear hunts for insects and mice.

The big bear crops several mouthfuls of grass and digs a few tiny bulbs. But she is not really hungry. Soon she and the cubs bed down again on a pile of leaves under a ledge of rock.

After a few days of activity the mother bear be-

16

comes very hungry. She keeps busy most of her waking hours, digging for bulbs and roots, cropping buds, leaves, and grass. She tears up rotten logs to search for fat beetle grubs, or to seize a scurrying mouse. She pounces on frogs at the woodland pond, and fishes for suckers in the stream. One day she finds the body of a yearling deer that did not survive the winter. Then she has a feast.

The bear does not follow any regular schedule in her hunting. Sometimes she is active during daylight hours. At other times she and the cubs wander about at night. They usually bed down at a different spot each time.

Day after day the bears wander through the woods, sometimes traveling several miles at a time. As yet the cubs do not eat any of the foods their mother does. But they nurse several times every day. Bellies full, they curl up and sleep after each feeding, humming contentedly to themselves.

Soon the mother bear's winter coat begins to come out in patches. Her appearance becomes ragged, and her skin itches. She scratches her back by rubbing herself against rough tree trunks.

As the cubs grow stronger they learn how to climb, and shinny high into the treetops. On the ground they wrestle and play with each other, often growling and bawling in mock anger. While their mother snoozes, they romp over her big comfortable body. Sometimes they nip at her ears. She is usually good-natured, but when the cubs nip too hard she growls a warning. If they keep it up, she cuffs them and sends them sprawling. The cubs must learn how to behave.

If possible danger threatens, all nonsense ends. Perhaps a dog barks in the distance. The mother bear sends the cubs scooting up into the safety of a tree, to stay until she calls them down. Perhaps they meet a skunk or a porcupine. The curious cubs want to investigate these strange animals, but their mother stops them with a grunt. The cubs need to learn what is dangerous and what is not, and their mother is their teacher.

One day in late June the three of them meet another black bear—a big male. The mother bear sends the cubs scrambling up a tree and then faces the male bear. He walks toward her, and she growls and snaps her jaws at him. She is telling him to go away. Male bears are not very good fathers. They sometimes kill small cubs. Finally the big male loses interest and wanders off.

During the summer, food is easy to find. The mother bear fills up on berries and other vegetable matter, with insects and mice for dessert. The cubs

18

Cubs soon learn to scramble up a tree when danger threatens.

begin to sample these foods, too. One lucky day their mother finds a bee tree. Then all three of them feast on honey.

Summer draws to an end and fall comes in with cool nights and brightly colored leaves. The cubs still drink their mother's milk, but now they are filling up on many other kinds of food as well. Their mother gorges on acorns and nuts, fruits and berries. Her plump body takes on a deep layer of fat, and her winter coat grows in thick and warm.

By the end of October the cubs weigh nearly 50

A mother black bear and her year-old cub. Bears in the same family often vary in color.

pounds apiece. They are fat, too, and as big as good-sized dogs. Before the first snowfall the bears start looking for a good den. This winter they sleep in a small cave with a narrow opening. Snuggled together on a bed of dried leaves, they doze off. Here they are secure against the storms of winter.

When spring comes at last, the bears leave their snug retreat. Once again they wander through the woods hunting for food. The young bears have big appetites this spring, for they are growing fast.

One day in June they again meet a big male bear. This time the mother bear does not chase him away. Instead, she leaves the youngsters and goes off with the male. She has found a mate. Seven months from now she will give birth to another pair of tiny cubs in her winter den.

The cubs are on their own now, but they are well able to look after themselves. They are strong and lanky, and each weighs close to 80 pounds. They stay together the rest of that summer and fall. Perhaps they den together that winter.

But when their third springtime comes the two-year-olds separate. Each wanders through the woods alone. The young bears are growing up. In a couple of years they may have cubs of their own.

3. American Black Bear

"Where are the bears?" the two boys ask as their father drives up to the south entrance of Yellowstone National Park in Wyoming. "We want to see some bears!"

A Park Ranger grins at them from the entrance booth. "You'll see plenty of bears before you get very far," he promises.

The boys peer out expectantly as they ride through the park—past Lewis Falls, past the gleaming silver waters of Yellowstone Lake. Half an hour passes before they spot their first bears—a fat, old female with two gangly cubs. They are standing calmly in the middle of the road, with cars lined up bumper to bumper on either side of them. Bears are protected in Yellowstone Park, and many of them have lost their fear of people.

Experienced panhandlers already, the two cubs are begging for food like dogs. Delighted tourists are obliging them with candy, popcorn, and sandwiches—whatever they have with them. Many people are standing in the road taking pictures of the bears at hardly more than arm's length. The boys take pictures, too—but their father makes them stay in the car to do it.

Finally their father drives on. Before the day is over, the boys have seen nearly 30 bears in all. They wouldn't have seen so many anywhere else.

Black bears are by far the commonest bears all over North America. Close to half a million of them roam the continent, from Alaska to northern Mexico, and from Labrador to Florida. In the United States alone there are probably 200,000 or more black bears. Hunters shoot about 20,000 of these every year.

Black bears live in every one of our heavily populated eastern states except Connecticut, Rhode Island, and Delaware. They are gone from several midwestern prairie states, too, but practically every other state boasts a thriving population. Alaska alone has an estimated 75,000 black bears, and each of the three West Coast states has about 20,000 of them. Half that many roam the forests and mountains of

24

North Carolina. Even New York State has close to 4000 bears.

Nearly 500 black bears live within the boundaries of Yellowstone, and about half that many roam Grand Teton National Park, just to the south. Glacier National Park in Montana and Great Smokies National Park in North Carolina have a couple of hundred black bears each.

In all of these parks, bears are one of the greatest

Black bears are a common sight for motorists in many national parks.

attractions. They *seem* as tame and friendly as big dogs. And that is the way many people think of them, despite park warnings not to feed the bears or get close to them. Every year a number of people get severely bitten, scratched, or mauled by park bears. These people are careless. They disobey park rules and get too close to the bears, or tease them. They forget that bears, even though they seem tame, are big and powerful wild animals.

A full-grown black bear stands from two and a half to three feet high at the shoulder. It measures four to six feet from the tip of its tan muzzle to the end of its stubby tail. The average weight is anywhere from 300 to 400 pounds, but record specimens have tipped the scales at 500 to 600 pounds, or even more.

Practically all the bears in eastern North America have black coats—sometimes with a small white V on the chest. But out West, the American black bear appears in many different colors, in spite of its name. Some are black, like their eastern brothers. Others are a deep chocolate brown. Still others have light reddish-tan coats. These are often called cinnamon bears. Any or all of these shades may occur in the same litter.

Two other quite different color types live in

coastal areas of Canada and Alaska. One, called the Glacier or blue bear, has a coat that ranges from blue-black to smoky gray-blue. It roams over a small coastal area of southern Alaska and northern British Columbia. The second type, called the Kermode's or white bear, lives on islands just to the south. Its coat is a distinctive whitish or cream color.

In spite of their appearance, both the Glacier and Kermode's bears are mere color varieties of the black bear. Their pelts are prized trophies to hunters, and both are becoming quite rare.

Whatever their color, black bears normally turn and skedaddle as fast as they can whenever they meet people in the wild. Even a mother bear with cubs usually runs away if she can. But if she is surprised or cornered, she may try to scare the intruder. She growls and champs her jaws together, clicking her teeth. This is usually just a bluff on her part. But if the intruder crowds his luck and advances toward her, she just *might* charge to protect her young. Don't try it!

Once in a great while black bears have been known to attack people in the wild, for no apparent good reason. There are even several instances of people being killed by them. But such attacks average less than one in every thousand.

27

The tall helmets worn by these guards at Buckingham Palace are made of Canadian black bear fur.

In some places black bears are nuisances for quite different reasons. They may develop a taste for mutton and become sheep-killers. In western forests they sometimes strip off and eat the bark of young Douglas fir trees. One bear can destroy hundreds of trees in this manner.

Bears have always been highly prized by man as game animals. In pioneer days, bear meat was a regular item of diet for many settlers. Bear fat was made into oil and used in cooking. It was also believed to be a good remedy for rheumatism and many other ailments. Bear pelts were used for bedding, or as thick warm robes. The tall fur helmets worn by royal guards at England's Buckingham Palace are still made of Canadian black bear fur.

Today, "Smokey Bear" is known throughout the United States as a guardian of our forests against careless fires. In blue jeans and forest-ranger hat, Smokey Bear warns us in thousands of signs that "Only you can prevent forest fires."

Smokey is a real bear—a cub that was rescued from a New Mexico forest fire in 1950 and sent to the National Zoological Park in Washington, D. C. He has been viewed by many hundreds of thousands of children there, and helped to educate millions of others all over the country.

"Smokey Bear" is often seen on posters warning campers to help prevent forest fires. The real Smokey (right) lives in the National Zoological Park in Washington, D. C.

Always hold
atches 'til cold

Be sure to
rown all fires

ush all smokes
dead out

follow
Smokey's ABC's...
Please! only you can

4. The Legendary Grizzly Bear

On June 14, 1805, Captain Meriwether Lewis and Lieutenant William Clark were camped near the Great Falls of the Missouri River, in what is now central Montana. Lewis and Clark were well into their famous expedition to explore the vast western wilderness which President Thomas Jefferson had recently purchased for the United States from France.

Lewis went out to hunt for fresh meat, and shot a buffalo. Before he could reload his gun a big grizzly bear came upon him, "open mouthed and full speed." There weren't any handy trees for him to climb, so Lewis was forced to run for his life. The bear gained on him, however, and Lewis in desperation waded into the Missouri River to his armpits. Much to his relief the bear didn't follow, so he lived to relate the incident in his journal.

This was not the party's first encounter with the grizzly, which Lewis and Clark often called the white bear or the brown bear, to distinguish it from the smaller black bear. Just a month before, six of the expedition's most experienced hunters had attacked a grizzly sleeping near the banks of the river. With four shots in its body the enraged giant stormed after its tormentors and scattered them, although it received at least two more rifle balls in the process. Two of the hunters escaped by canoe, while the others hid in bushes along the shore. The rampaging bear routed them out, and two of them jumped into the river to escape. But the determined animal went right in after them! A shot through its head finally killed it. Afterward, the hunters counted eight different shots in its body.

"The wonderful power of life which these animals possess renders them dreadful . . ." Lewis recorded. ". . . we had rather encounter two Indians than meet a single brown bear." Largest and most powerful of all the meat-eating animals in the western mountains, the grizzly seemed to fear nothing, including man, in those early days.

A few western traders and mountain men had encountered grizzlies before this time, but Lewis

A grizzly bear. Much larger than the black bear, the grizzly has a "dished-out" face, a shoulder hump, and longer claws.

and Clark were the first to write detailed accounts of the big bear's appearance and characteristics. They shot the specimen from which the original scientific description was made some years later. Reading their accounts, the man who gave the grizzly its scientific name called it *Ursus horribilis,* "horrible bear."

The average grizzly stands three to three and a

half feet at the shoulder, measures six or seven feet in length, and weighs 500 to 800 pounds. Big individuals may approach 1000 pounds or more.

Much larger than the black bear, the grizzly differs from its smaller cousin in various other ways. Black bears have straight noses, while grizzly bears have bulging brows that give their profiles a "dished out" or concave appearance. The grizzly has a noticeable shoulder hump while the black bear does not. Grizzlies have much longer claws than black bears—up to four or five inches long on the front feet. They are not as curved as the claws of the black bear, however.

The grizzly's fur varies from very light tan or yellowish to almost black. Many individuals have light-tipped hair, or light hair mixed with the dark, giving their fur a frosted effect. Such a grizzly is often called a "silvertip." Others have a light face contrasting with a dark body, giving them the name "baldface grizzly."

The long powerful claws make the grizzly an expert digger. It may plow up a whole hillside in an afternoon, digging for roots and bulbs or searching for burrowing rodents. Occasionally the grizzly kills a large animal such as an elk. Then, after eating its fill, it may drag the body to some sheltered spot and cover it with dirt or brush. It is hiding it away for a future meal.

Grizzly bears mature when they are three to five years old, and the female gives birth to cubs no oftener than every other year. The winter shelter in which the cubs are born may be a cave or natural opening in a rock ledge, but sometimes the mother bear digs out a roomy sleeping den for herself in a hillside. The cubs usually stay with their mothers until they are at least a year and a half old.

A century and a half ago, grizzly bears inhabited practically all of our western states. They lived mainly in mountains and forests, but some roamed desert areas, too. A few even ranged over the plains as far east as the Dakotas and Nebraska.

Western pioneers such as Lewis and Clark recorded the first vivid encounters with grizzly bears in the Rocky Mountains. But Spanish settlers of California and the Southwest had already been familiar with grizzly bears for many years.

In California, daredevil Spanish cowboys or *vaqueros* practiced a hair-raising sport with grizzly bears just for the thrill of it. They lassoed the bears from horseback. Usually working in teams of four or more, the Spaniards would surround a bear. Then one of them would toss a lariat around one

35

of the bear's legs. Pulling the rope tight, the successful horseman would keep his distance from the bear while another man roped a second leg and pulled in the opposite direction. Finally, if luck was with them, the cowboys had the bear spread-eagled and helpless. After being bound and gagged, the victim was loaded on a sling pulled by oxen and hauled back to the ranch, or to town.

Here, the captive grizzly was often used in a cruel and brutal activity—bear-and-bull baiting.

"Roping the Bear" by James Walker. The painting shows several nooses around the animal's neck, but usually the grizzly was roped around each foot.

Chained to a post in an arena, the bear was matched against a wild Spanish bull while cheering crowds watched and bet on the probable winner. The bear usually won such bloody contests, but once in a while the bull would kill the bear with a desperate thrust of its long, sharp horns. Bear-baiting was still popular during the California gold rush days of 1848 and 1849. By the 1860's, however, it was finally outlawed in most places.

These years also include one of the most amazing

chapters in the long and exciting history of man and grizzly bear. This is the story of John Capen Adams, better known as "Grizzly Adams." Born in Medway, Massachusetts in 1807, Adams started out in life as a shoemaker. Later he turned to trapping wild animals in Vermont, and then to working with an early circus.

An adventuresome and restless spirit, Adams headed West in 1848 and several years later became a wild animal hunter and trapper in the Sierra Nevada Mountains of California.

Although he hunted grizzly bears with rare skill and zest, and killed many of them, Adams is known best for the grizzly bears which he captured as cubs, then reared and tamed. His first pet grizzly was a young female, some months old when he captured her. He named this bear "Lady Washington," in honor of the United States' first First Lady. Using a mixture of firmness, friendliness, and good sense, he tamed Lady Washington so that she bore packs on her back and accompanied him on his hunting trips.

Even more of a friend was "Ben Franklin," a grizzly cub that Adams captured when it was just a few days old. Adams' greyhound dog Rambler had just given birth to pups, and he induced her

Grizzly Adams with his favorite companion, "Ben Franklin."

to nurse the tiny cub. As Ben grew up, a close bond developed between him and his master. Adams called Ben Franklin "the flower of his race, my firmest friend, the boon companion of my after-years."

Soon Ben was accompanying Adams on nearly all of his trips through the mountains. On one occasion the faithful pet saved Adams' life by attacking a wild grizzly that was mauling his master. With Ben's help, Adams managed to crawl free, pick up his rifle and shoot the wild grizzly. But both Adams and Ben were considerably "chawed up" in the encounter. After they had painfully made their way back to camp, Adams bound up Ben's wounds before he did anything for his own.

In 1856 Grizzly Adams gave up his wild and adventurous life in the mountains and settled in San Francisco. Here he started a museum and wild animal exhibit which featured Lady Washington and Ben Franklin, among others. Faithful Ben Franklin died in 1858, and a San Francisco newspaper lamented his passing in an editorial entitled "Death of a Distinguished Native Californian."

Adams packed up his menagerie early in 1860 and headed for New York, sailing around Cape Horn in a sailing vessel, "The Golden Fleece." In

Manhattan the old grizzly-bear tamer signed a contract with P. T. Barnum, the leading showman of his day. For some months he captivated New Yorkers with his huge and generally amiable bears, after parading them up Broadway on horse-drawn wagons as an advertisement for his show.

Adams had been attacked and wounded by grizzlies many times during his years in the West. Sick and failing, he nevertheless courageously showed his bears until a few days before his death in the fall of 1860. Today he lies buried in Massachusetts, the native state to which he finally returned.

5. A Vanishing Monarch

In Grizzly Adams' day, grizzly bears ranged over practically all of our western states. The region was mostly wilderness at that time. But after gold was discovered in California in 1848, the trickle of western pioneers and settlers quickly became a torrent. Farmers and cattlemen and adventurers of every type poured into the western lands to stake their claims. Everywhere they went, they killed grizzly bears on sight. From that day until this, the grizzly's range and numbers have steadily become smaller and smaller.

The grizzly was too dangerous an animal to be tolerated close to settlements. More and more of the land was being taken over for farms and ranches, too, and grizzlies got a bad reputation as stock killers in many areas.

One famous renegade bear, "Old Mose," was credited with killing at least 800 cattle and five men in Colorado. His tracks could always be identified because two toes were missing on his left hind foot. A $1000 reward was posted for his scalp, and experienced hunters and trappers all over the West vowed to collect it.

But for many years the bear outwitted all of his enemies. It was not until 1904 that a pack of hunting dogs finally brought him to bay. Closing in, the dogs' master killed Old Mose—but it took eight bullets to finish him.

Grizzly bears were quite common in California in 1846, when the settlers were fighting for their independence from Mexico. In recognition of their territory's most fearsome wild animal, the California settlers designed a flag that featured the grizzly bear.

Today the grizzly bear still appears on the California state flag, and is listed as the official state animal. The University of California claims the grizzly as its mascot or symbol, and its athletic teams are nicknamed "Bruins" or "Golden Bears." But now there are no more wild grizzlies at all in California, the Bear State. The last reported grizzly bear in California was shot in 1922.

44

Grizzlies are fast disappearing from most of North America. But a good number can still be found in the wilderness of Alaska and western Canada.

The story of the grizzly's disappearance in other western states is very much the same. Today probably no more than 500 grizzly bears live in all of the United States south of Canada. About 200 of these live within the protected boundaries of Yellowstone National Park. Perhaps half that many roam Glacier National Park in Montana. A very few grizzlies still survive in remaining wilderness areas of Montana, Wyoming, and Idaho. Washington and Colorado list about 10 animals each. Every year the pitifully small total shrinks a bit. The grizzly's day in the United States outside of Alaska seems to be almost over.

The same story holds true in Mexico, where perhaps 30 grizzlies still live in remote mountainous areas of the state of Chihuahua.

Grizzlies are hard pressed in northern North America, too, but a good number of them still roam wilderness strongholds of western Canada and Alaska. Recent studies indicate between 8000 and 12,000 grizzlies and big brown bears living in Alaska, and at least that many in the Canadian Rockies.

But even here the grizzly's wilderness domain is shrinking fast. Unless the bears are protected in time, they eventually face the same fate in the North as in areas farther to the south.

One bright spot is the report on the Tundra or Barren Ground grizzly—a race that lives on the treeless barrens of far northern Canada. Once considered almost extinct, the Barren Ground bear is slowly increasing its population, and seems to be extending its range eastward toward Hudson Bay.

Today, grizzlies are not as quick to attack man as they were a century or two ago. The bears seem to have learned from bitter experience to fear man and his guns. But don't count on it! Grizzly bears may still attack when provoked.

Experts in grizzly-bear psychology advise making plenty of noise when traveling through bear country. Let the grizzlies know you are coming, so they have a chance to slip away. If you stumble on a grizzly by accident, avoid sudden movements. Don't advance toward the bear. Give it the opportunity to make up its mind to move on, and chances are it will.

But if the bear happens to be in a surly mood and comes for you, climb a tree if you can and wait for help to come.

Two wildlife experts, Frank and John Craighead, have recently been studying grizzly bears in Yellowstone National Park. The Craigheads trap grizzlies in culvert traps, then "shoot" them with a needle filled with a muscle-relaxing drug. This makes the bears helpless for a little while, but does not harm them. The bears are measured, ear-tagged, and sometimes tattooed with a number. Some of them get plastic collars of different colors for future identification. Some are fitted with tiny radio transmit-

ters by which they can be tracked as they roam their regular ranges.

In this way the Craigheads expect to learn more about the typical grizzly bear's movements, what it eats, where and when it dens up in winter, and other facts which will help in grizzly management and conservation.

Wildlife experts John and Frank Craighead capture grizzlies in traps made of culvert pipe (top left), then inject them with a drug. While they are helpless, they are weighed (bottom left), measured, and tagged for future identification. Some are fitted with a special collar that sends radio signals (below) so they can be followed as they roam their ranges.

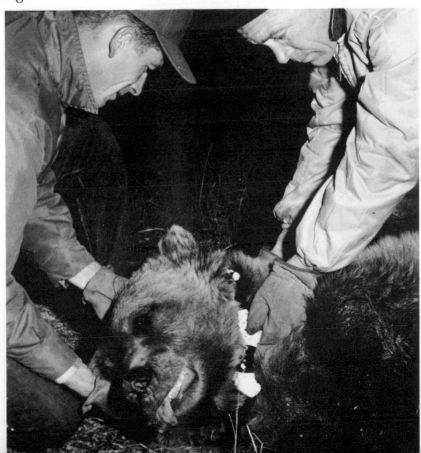

6. Alaska's Big Brown Bears

A huge brown bear wades into a swift-flowing stream and peers intently at the swirling, foam-flecked waters. Suddenly a giant paw flashes downward, pinning something to the bottom. Then down goes the massive head. When it comes up again, a two-foot-long salmon is flopping between the massive jaws.

Carrying his prize ashore, the big brownie strips the firm pink flesh from the fish and gulps it down. Overhead a flock of gulls wheel on outstretched wings, waiting to snatch up the scraps.

Finished with his first course, the shaggy fisherman wades out to catch another salmon. This stretch of stream is his regular fishing grounds. A short distance upstream, four other giant bears are also feasting on salmon. Downstream are two she-

An Alaskan brown bear wades into a swift stream (above), captures a salmon in its powerful jaws (right top), and takes it ashore for a meal.

bears with cubs. The cubs wait impatiently on the bank while their mothers catch their dinner for them.

Giant brown bears such as these live on islands and coastal areas from Unimak Island off the western tip of the Alaska Peninsula to the coastal islands of northern British Columbia. They are the biggest land carnivores on earth. Males often weigh 1000

pounds, and several record specimens of more than 1600 pounds have been reported. The hind-foot print of such a bear may measure 14 inches long and 8 inches wide. Females average smaller—but all of them are *big* bears!

These giant brown bears of Alaska look very much like huge grizzlies. They don't have the grizzly's prominent shoulder hump, however, and their fur is generally darker and a more even color. The claws of the big brownies are somewhat shorter and more curved, and their heads are generally more massive.

Even with these differences, it takes an expert to tell a big brown bear from a grizzly. The bears themselves don't worry about the differences, and all sorts of gradations between the two types exist. Today, most students of mammals consider that grizzlies and Alaskan brown bears, as well as the smaller brown bears of Europe and Asia, are merely different races of one wide-ranging species.

The bears that live on Kodiak Island, just south of the Alaska Peninsula, are among the largest of the Alaskan brown bears. They are called Kodiak bears. Kodiak is famous for its bears, and a large portion of the island has been set aside as a refuge for them.

Kodiak bears are among the largest of the Alaskan brown bears.

Another variety just about as big lives on the Alaska mainland, to the north. It is called the Peninsula bear. Both Peninsula and Kodiak bears are generally dusky brown in color. But the bears of Admiralty Island, several hundred miles to the south, are almost black. Altogether, at least eight different races of Alaskan brown bears are recognized.

In winter, big brown bears generally retire to a cave or den dug in a slope. Most of them hole up by late November. Adult males usually emerge from their long winter sleep in April, but females with cubs wait until early May before they appear. At this time of year the bears usually spend some time on the mountain slopes, eating grass or digging for roots and bulbs. They use the same paths year after year, and their well-worn trails crisscross back and forth on the hillsides.

Once salmon start their yearly run upstream to spawning beds, the big brown bears gather in areas close to good streams. Each adult bear stakes out his private fishing area. The bears gorge on salmon throughout most of the summer, putting on thick layers of fat to sustain them through the long winter. In late summer they often vary their diet with berries. By November it is time to den up again.

To big game hunters, Alaska's giant brown bears are one of the world's most prized trophies. In order to keep their population at a safe level, however, the number of bears shot each season must be strictly controlled. Every year the big brownies are feeling more and more the press of people and civilization on their northern homeland.

Vast lumbering operations on Admiralty Island threaten the bears' habitat there. Ranchers on Kodiak Island grumble because the bears sometimes dine on livestock. Commercial fishermen say that the bears everywhere are eating too many salmon. The big brown fish-eaters have been dining on salmon for thousands of years, however, and during all that time the salmon have flourished.

Alaska's big brown bears need suitable refuges and protection if we don't want them to go the way of the grizzlies in our western states.

7. *Polar Bear of the North*

A fat seal lies snoozing beside its hole on the Arctic ice pack. Some distance away, a hungry polar bear spies the sleek dark form and creeps toward it.

The seal blinks and lifts its head to peer about for possible danger. Instantly the polar bear crouches motionless, as if carved of ice. The seal does not see it. Reassured, the fat, web-footed animal goes back to sleep. Again the white bear begins its slow stalking—nearer, nearer.

Finally the bear is close enough. It charges, swift and deadly. A huge paw hammers downward, and the seal dies before it even realizes that the enemy is upon it.

The polar bear, "Nanook" to the Eskimos, looks quite different from other bears. The long neck,

small head, close-set ears, and little beady eyes combine to give its face an almost weasel-like appearance. The thick shaggy coat is nearly snow-white during the winter, but sometimes takes on a yellowish tinge in summer. The black soles of the huge feet are furred, giving Nanook non-skid footwear for traveling over ice and snow.

Polar bears rival Alaskan brown bears in size. Big males stand four to four and a half feet high at the shoulder, measure nine feet in length, and weigh as much as 1000 pounds or more. The biggest one ever weighed tipped the scales at 1728 pounds. That is the greatest weight ever recorded for any bear.

Nanook roams the polar ice cap all around the northern hemisphere, mainly above the Arctic Circle. Its best hunting grounds are in areas where huge ice fields break up to meet the frigid waters of the Arctic Ocean. That's where the white bear finds its favorite prey, the seal.

In winter, polar bears sometimes drift far southward with the advancing ice fields. At times they range far out to sea on jagged cakes of ice. As the ice recedes each summer, the bears retreat northward. And since the great Arctic ice fields are constantly, though very slowly, drifting, an individual

61

With its long neck, small head, and shaggy white coat, the polar bear looks quite different from other bears.

bear may be north of Alaska one year, far above Greenland or Siberia another year. They are international in their movements.

Powerful swimmers, polar bears may travel many miles through the water as they move from one ice floe to another one. Cubs swim alongside their mother, but if they become tired they simply seize the fur of her back or rump in their teeth. Then she tows them along behind her.

The most carnivorous of all bears, Nanook usually stalks its prey over the ice. A very keen sense of smell helps the bear locate its next meal. So does its eyesight, which is considerably sharper than that of other bears. As the huge bear creeps toward a victim, its shaggy white coat helps to conceal it against the snowy background.

Sometimes, if a seal is lying close to open water, the bear secures its favorite meal in another way. Swimming beneath the ice field, the bear strikes the ice near the seal's blowhole. The alarmed seal dives through its escape hatch for safety. But the polar bear is in the water below, waiting to seize it.

King of all its icy domain, the great white sea bear has little to fear from any other land animal except man. In the water it sometimes falls victim to hungry killer whales, or a herd of enraged walruses.

Whenever it has the opportunity, the polar bear will try to creep up on a herd of dozing walruses and make off with a baby. But woe to the bear if the walrus herd awakes to the loss in time. A walrus can swim faster than a bear, and its long ivory tusks can pierce the bear through and through.

To vary their meat diet, polar bears sometimes

Adult polar bears are powerful swimmers, as much at home in the water as on land.

eat grass or other sparse Arctic vegetation in springtime. They gulp down eggs of seabirds, too, and
capture waterfowl by swimming underwater and
seizing them from below. Once in a while a beached
whale furnishes a feast lasting days for a whole
troop of hungry bears.

Adult male polar bears almost never visit land.
They remain on the drift ice—their favorite hunting
grounds—the year through. Except for females
expecting young, polar bears do not den up to
sleep during the long, dark Arctic winter. They are
on the move all the time, hunting for food.

Female bears expecting cubs come ashore in the
fall. Sometimes they travel many miles inland. Finding a southern-facing slope where the snow is deep,
they dig out a spacious sleeping chamber. Drifting
snow soon covers the den, except for a small breath-
ing hole.

Here, snug and warm, the female gives birth to
cubs in late November or early December. The
cubs are only about 10 inches long and develop
slowly. Their eyes do not open until they are about
six weeks old.

Leaving the den in late March or early April, the
mother leads her youngsters to the sea. She begins
to hunt once more, and the cubs learn the ways of

In the wild, this polar bear cub would be born in a snowy cave on a
hillside. When her cubs are about four months old, their mother
leads them to the sea.

the Arctic world. They remain with her until their second summer.

Years ago, the only human hunters of polar bears were the Eskimos. The great white bears were prized quarry, for they supplied these natives of the far north with warm fur robes, much good meat and fat. Polar bear hunts were dangerous affairs in those days, for the Eskimos were armed only with spears or harpoons. Any member of the tribe who killed one of the great white bears was honored for his bravery. Many hunters paid for their courage with their lives.

Today most Eskimo hunters are equipped with high-powered rifles. These modern weapons make it much easier to kill the bears. Another threat to Nanook is the increasing use of airplanes that take hunters out over the Arctic ice in search of bears. When a polar bear is spotted the plane lands. Sometimes all the hunter needs to do is step outside and shoot it. Today an estimated 1000 to 1300 polar bears are killed around the world each year.

With such a toll, many people are afraid that the polar bear will soon disappear. A scientist who has studied them recently believes that there are less than 20,000 polar bears left in the world. If the population is that small, it may not be able to stand such a yearly hunting pressure.

In the fall of 1965, scientists from the five countries most affected—the United States, Canada, Denmark, Norway, and Russia—gathered in Fairbanks, Alaska, to consider the plight of the polar bear. They recommended stricter hunting laws to help safeguard the bears, and continued study of their habits.

It will be sad if the time comes when the only polar bears left are those in zoos. Most of us may never see them roaming their Arctic homeland, but it is nice to know that they are there.

8. Bears of Other Lands

A brightly-clothed gypsy wanders down a dirt road in a remote mountainous area of Turkey. A shaggy brown bear shuffles along behind him, like a big dog on a leash. In a little village the gypsy stops and puts on a show with his tame bear.

The big, slow-moving beast stands up and dances in time to the clang of the gypsy's tambourine. It turns somersaults and plays with a ball. It wrestles with the man, and begs for food. Finally the performance is finished, and the spectators toss a few coins into the gypsy's cap.

The gypsy's amiable pet is an Old World brown bear—the kind of bear most commonly tamed and used in circus acts. Performing brown bears quickly learn many different tricks. Many of them climb

71

ladders and walk tightropes. A few even learn how to ride on motorcycles!

Long ago, Old World brown bears roamed most of Europe and Asia. As the land became thickly populated and cultivated, however, they disappeared in many regions. Small numbers still survive in wild and mountainous areas of Spain, Greece, and the Balkan countries. A few still roam the Alps and the forests of Scandinavia. But most of the world's remaining brown bears live in Russia and northern Asia.

In different parts of its range the brown bear's color varies from light tan to almost black. The size also varies from region to region, but all Old World brown bears average somewhat smaller than American grizzlies and brown bears. All three are very much alike, however.

Asia is also the home of three kinds of bears which are found nowhere else—the Asiatic black bear, the sloth bear, and the Malayan sun bear.

The Asiatic black bear is sometimes called the Moon bear, because of the large whitish crescent that marks its chest. A forest dweller, it is a shaggy black animal that seldom grows much heavier than 300 pounds. It has large fringed ears, and long hair that forms a sort of a cape on its shoulders. It ranges

73

A gypsy and his trained dancing bear.

through forest and mountain areas from Afghanistan eastward through the Himalayas to Indochina, and northward through China to Siberia and Japan.

The sloth bear lives in the jungles of India and Ceylon. It is also called the honey bear. Covered with long black or brownish fur, it has a short mane and a light-colored V or Y on its chest. The sloth

The sloth, or honey, bear is found in the jungles of India and Ceylon.

bear has exceptionally long claws and a long mobile snout. Its principal food consists of fruit, eggs, insects, and other small animals. Finding a termite nest or ant hill, the sloth bear tears it open with its long claws, then vacuums up the swarming insects with its long tongue and sucking lips. Honey is a favorite food, too.

The Malayan sun bear is the smallest bear. This one is just a cub.

The Malayan sun bear is the smallest of all bears. Seldom weighing much more than 100 pounds, it has a sleek coat of shiny black hair, and a prominent orange or yellowish breast mark. The sun bear ranges from Burma and Indochina southward through Malaya, Sumatra, and Borneo. Living in tropical regions, it does not hibernate. An agile climber, it eats fruit, honey, and whatever small animals it can catch.

The only bear found in South America is the little-known spectacled bear. A rather small bear with a blackish coat, it is named for the ring of light hair that surrounds each eye. Living from western Venezuela and Columbia southward to Peru and Bolivia, it roams the forests of the high Andes at heights of 7000 to 9000 feet. Mainly a vegetarian, the spectacled bear is particularly fond of palm fruit. When it wants to snooze, it is said to build resting platforms or nests of sticks and branches high in the treetops.

The giant panda of Asia is a close relative of all the true bears. Except for its contrasting black and white color pattern it looks very much like a bear— so much so that early naturalists called it the "particolored bear." Some scientists, even today, include it as a member of the bear family. Others argue that

76

The rings of light-colored fur around its eyes give the spectacled bear its name.

it is closer related to the raccoons.

Weighing 300 pounds or more when full grown, the giant panda has a stocky bearlike body, short powerful legs, and a tiny stub tail. Most of its body is white, but its legs are black, and so is a saddle over the shoulders. Black ears and black rings around the eyes contrast with the appealing white face.

The giant panda was unknown to the western world until 1869, when the adventurous priest-naturalist, Father David, discovered it in the remote mountains of western Szechwan Province in China. A rather sluggish animal, the giant panda is an expert climber. A vegetarian, it eats only the leaves and shoots of bamboo. Although it lives in a cool climate, it does not den up and sleep through the winter, as the majority of bears do.

The first giant panda ever seen alive in the Western Hemisphere was brought to America in 1936. Eight others were brought in during the next five years, and exhibited at New York's Bronx Zoo, the Chicago Brookfield Zoo, and the St. Louis Zoo. Today, however, there are no giant pandas in America. Outside of China, the only specimens in captivity are a female in the London Zoo and a male in the Moscow Zoo.

78

The giant panda's rarity and striking appearance have made it a favorite with people all over the world.

Bears are great favorites with people everywhere, too. And anyone can see bears in the nearest zoo, if not in the wild. These big shaggy animals can be as playful as puppies, or as dignified as great Uncle Herbert. In turn they can be friendly or disgruntled, curious or disdainful, dainty or greedy, timid or bold. Bears have lots of personality, and that's probably the reason people like them so much.

"Chi-Chi," at the London Zoo, is one of only two giant pandas in captivity outside China. The other one lives in the Moscow Zoo.

INDEX

80

About the Author

ROBERT McCLUNG is the author of more than twenty books for boys and girls, including *The Swift Deer, Mammals and How They Live,* and *All About Animals and Their Young.*

His experience in working with animals makes Mr. McClung especially well qualified to write about them for young people. He was on the staff of New York's famed Bronx Zoo for seven years, rising to the position of Curator of Mammals and Birds. He has also been a book editor for the National Geographic Society, working on such volumes as *Wild Animals of North America.*

Mr. McClung holds a B.A. degree in biology from Princeton University, and an M.A. in zoology from Cornell. He lives with his wife and two sons in Amherst, Massachusetts.